Implications & Distinctions

Implications & Distinctions

Format, Content and Context in Contemporary Race Film

A text by Martine Syms

Future Plan and Program

1. Say it Loud

In my short career I've been asked to publicly dissect my practice in terms of race at least ten times. Each time I paused. I had to both find and fix this color line, no matter how ambiguous its parameters seemed, because it matters to people both Black and White. Embracing a definition of ethnicity lets us feel as though we understand one another. I once overheard someone expressing his frustration after a Rashid Johnson lecture. "He would not talk about being Black, but he uses Black people and cocoa butter in his work!" Johnson can't depict Black people without it being noteworthy because the dominant voice of mainstream America is decidedly White. Not only are Black people implicated as Other, but artifacts of their experience are involved as well. Suddenly cocoa butter, basketball, collard greens and gospel music are Black too. It doesn't matter if those things are being manufactured and marketed by non-Blacks. Being an Other is complicated. By examining what Blackness can mean for filmmakers in terms of production, distribution and exhibition I will have an answer the next time I'm interrogated.

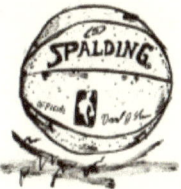 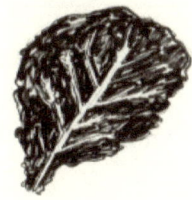

Artifacts of the Black American experience

Previous reflections on Black cinema have focused their efforts on outlining the positive and negative aspects of these finite portrayals. I'd like to join the conversation of historians who are looking at the ways that Blackness has been visualized. I choose to discuss moving images because they are pervasive. Video artist Nam June Paik is rumored to have said "the culture that's going to survive in the future is the culture that you can carry around in your head." I carry movies in my head: pieces of dialogue, melodies from soundtracks, a wide establishing shot with titles in front. When I was little I asked my mom to do my hair like my cousin's, who I imagine asked her mom to do her hair like Janet Jackson in *Poetic Justice* (1993). We are the images we eat. In the same way that a cosmetic like High Time's Bump Stopper can be Black, a film can be Black. We know it when we see it, but can it be defined? What does a Black film look like and what does it sound like?

A "Black voice" might be the same as an "African-American voice," or even a "Negro voice." I identify as Black because I have no connection to Africa and it seems disingenuous to claim one. I also relate "-American" to immigration. If my parents had emigrated from Africa and I was born in America, I would adopt the African-American label. However, I am the descendant of slaves. My family's history is largely undocumented and further confused by acts of self-determination. My last name, Syms, was changed from Simms by my great-great-grandfather. Simms was the name of a slave owner. At our family reunion we all agreed to be united under the surname Graham-Macintosh, but I have no idea who Graham/Macintosh were, or where they

1 Jafa, "69."

came from. "We were never immigrants," as Dr. Vivian said to Sylvia Landry in the 1920 Oscar Micheaux release *Within Our Gates*.

This notion of displacement finds its way into many Black narratives, from Whoopi Goldberg as a fugitive lounge singer in *Sister Act* (1992), to Will Smith's on-screen arrival as "The Fresh Prince of Bel-Air," to Sun Ra's galactic adventures in *Space Is the Place* (1974). In her 2008 short, *The Fullness of Time*, experimental filmmaker Cauleen Smith combines the metaphorical displacement of Afrofuturism with the true stories of Hurricane Katrina survivors in New Orleans to create a lyrical trip through time and place. During the Q&A following a recent screening, Smith was asked what motivated her to devote an entire section of the video to a church sermon.[2] In the scene, the protagonist enters a storefront church, takes a seat in the back and listens to the pastor's sermon until she is moved to tears.

Smith decided to include the extended oration in response to the twenty-second clip of Pastor Jeremiah Wright proclaiming "goddamn America" that was being circulated at the time. "The minute I saw that clip I knew it was taken out of context," she explained, "If you tell the congregation at a Black church that everything is good and that everything is going to be alright they won't believe you. Black preachers have to guide their congregation through anger, through frustration ... They have to take them on this journey and then lift them up to God. Then they have to let them down very, very gently, so that everyone

2 Smith, "Carousel Microcinema 4.2."

can leave and get through the rest of their week." Smith then went on to describe how the moment of exhalation was so palpable that her actor really cried, "Troi wasn't acting in that scene. She was just *at church*."

The process of the Black preaching tradition that Smith describes is very similar to the classical narrative structure that is taught in film school. It begins with an introduction to the characters and setting, conflict emerges and gives way to rising action culminating in a climactic moment, which then falls into a resolution. On the website Soul Preaching, George Larry writes that the Black preaching style comes from "a mindset that is born in the unique experience of being the outcasts of society."[3] And from that experience also comes the race film.

Until the late forties the term "race film," like "race record," was used by the entertainment industry to describe an American production made for a Black audience by Black artists. I continue to use the term to distinguish this activity from the dominant Hollywood film business. In his "No-Theory Theory of Black Cinema," Tommy Lott asserts that Black films belong to the Third Cinema tradition because they contribute to the "advancement of Black people, within a context of systematic denial."[4] I would argue that the Third Cinema movement was unsuccessful and that the most politically subversive films available today are dismissed as "B-movies." Race film is not a genre, but a paradigm for filmmaking that is related to B-movie

3 Larry, "Black Preaching Myths – Is it Only For Black People?"

4 *Representing Blackness*, 93.

practices. A B-movie is categorized as such because of a low production budget, a lack of "A-list" actors and strong generic allegiances. The term was originally used to identify commercial films that were intended to be shown as the less publicized half of a double feature. B-movies are not critically acclaimed, and they do not win Oscars. In the past this was an obstacle for filmmakers, but in the long-tail distribution market a film can be released directly to its audience.

The quality of race films, like that of B-movies, ranges drastically, but I'm not concerned with making judgments about the merits of each film. What connects these disparate works are their methods of production and distribution. Regardless of whether or not a race film is "good," it will be treated by the film industry as a second-tier picture. Spike Lee talks at length about his struggle against Hollywood studios in his books *Do The Right Thing* and *By Any Means Necessary*. Despite successful box office performances, race films are routinely given budgets far below the average mainstream picture. The theatrical distribution of race films is also much more limited than that of other films.

2. High Drama

Precious: Based on the Novel Push by Sapphire was made independently by director Lee Daniels on a modest three million dollar budget that was later increased by executive producers Tyler Perry and Oprah Winfrey. The film won three awards at the Sundance Film Festival, and received a fifteen-minute standing ovation at the Cannes Film Festival. *Precious* was picked up for distribution by Lionsgate and opened on November 6, 2009 in 18 theaters.[5] *The Men Who Stare at Goats*, a comedic adaptation with a nearly all White cast, also opened on November 6, 2009 in 2,443 theaters.[6]

Precious is about an illiterate, obese girl named Claireece 'Precious' Jones, who is twice impregnated by her father and abused by her mother, but is encouraged by a light-skinned teacher to continue her education. The film is strongly informed by the politics of racial uplift, an ideology that naively equates a Black person's moral and material progress with increased social acceptance. In a biting review for the *New York Press*, Armond White wrote "These two media titans—plus one shrewd pathology pimp—use *Precious* to rework Booker T.

5 "Box Office Mojo."

6 Ibid.

Washington's early 20th-century manifesto *Up From Slavery* into extreme drama for the new millennium: Up From Incest, Child Abuse, Teenage Pregnancy, Poverty and AIDS."[7] While I don't agree with White's personal attacks against Perry, Winfrey and Daniels, he recognizes that *Precious* is an update on the familiar Black-themed uplifting drama.

During her career Winfrey has produced a slew of uplifting dramas for big and small screens. Her most ambitious works are *The Color Purple* (1985) and *Beloved* (1998). Both films are screen adaptations of literary works by Alice Walker and Toni Morrison respectively. *The Color Purple* deals with pre-war racism in the South through the lens of an abused young woman, while *Beloved* considers the Reconstruction era in Ohio from the perspective of a former slave. *The Color Purple* is the type of movie you put on to have a good cry. It's a sweeping drama full of movie magic, thoroughly removed of the discomfort that underscores Walker's novel. William Joyner of the *New York Times* remarked, "A look back at that accomplished, if melodramatic, film illustrates just how different a Hollywood vehicle ''Beloved'' is for the literary-cinematic consideration of America's racial history, and perhaps how different 1998 is from 1985."[8] During promotional publicity Oprah referred to the film as her "*Schindler's List.*"[9] Hollywood saw *Beloved* as an experiment to see whether or not big-budget, dramatic,

7 White. "Pride & Precious."

8 Joyner, "Staying Stubbornly True to a Writer's Vision."

9 Weinraub, "'Beloved' Tests Racial Themes At Box Office; Will This Winfrey Fim Appeal to White Audiences?"

Black-themed movies were a good investment. The film was a commercial failure that grossed less than half of its eighty million dollar budget. The graphic depiction of slavery, murder and Thandie Newton's terrifying performance as the drooling, rasping Beloved was enough to make any audience squirm. Although Oprah clearly has crossover appeal, her works fit squarely within the conventions that were codified by Oscar Micheaux's early race dramas.

Michaeux was a homesteader who wrote and published a book based on his life, and sold it door-to-door. After record-breaking success in publishing, Micheaux was approached by the Johnson Brothers of the Lincoln Motion Picture Company in Los Angeles, to turn the book into a movie. Lincoln was the first commercially successful producer of Black films. Dissatisfied with the way the Johnson Brothers were handling the production, Micheaux founded the Micheaux Book and Film Company and began working on the film himself. *The Homesteader* was completed in 1919, making it the first feature film released by a Black production company. The semi-autobiographical film tells of a young man, Jean Baptiste (Charles Lucas), who moves from Chicago to South Dakota and falls in love with a white woman, Agnes Stewart (Iris Hall). Disheartened, he returns to Chicago and marries Orlean (Evelyn Preer), the daughter of a preacher. When their miserable union ends, Jean goes back to South Dakota where he discovers that Agnes is Black. They marry and the story ends.

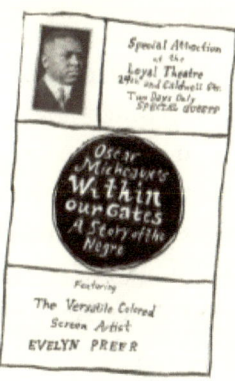

Micheaux was a skilled movie marketer

Micheaux's films espoused the values of the Black middle class, while still catering to popular sensationalism. *The Homesteader* was advertised with a tabloid style headline that read "SHOULD RACES INTERMARRY?"[10] This approach allowed Micheaux to compete with Hollywood studios well into the sound era, completing more than forty films before his death in 1951. In his didactic films, Micheaux tackled the conflicting ideas of "progress" that plagued Black communities during the Great Migration from the rural south to the urban north. Micheaux's work both established and defined the canon of race drama. After Micheaux, filmmakers working in this tradition appropriate his belief that they are not representatives of the Black perspective, instead they provide pedagogical expression for the Black community.[11]

The contemporary analog to Oscar Micheaux is mainstream auteur Tyler Perry. Perry began his career with a

10 Cripps, *Slow Fade to Black*, 184.

11 Stewart, *Migrating to the Movies*, 219.

series of plays focused on religious, working-class Black women, most notably a character named Madea, an elderly woman who dispensed tough love. His shows toured the "Chitlin' Circuit" in the nineties, and he cultivated a devout following among the religious, working class Black women he claims to represent. The plays were recorded and bootleg DVDs found their way into many Black homes, mine included. Tyler Perry was able to turn his modest productions into a multi-million dollar business. His twenty-odd films have grossed more than four hundred million dollars, yet he remains stuck in a Hollywood ghetto. Perry is billed as the writer, director and producer of all of his films. He even performs in drag to adopt the persona of Madea. In response to recent criticism Perry told CBS, "Let me tell you what Madea, Brown, all these characters are are [sic] bait. Disarming, charming, make-you-laugh bait, so I can slap Madea in something and talk about God, love, faith, forgiveness, family, any of those things, you know."[12]

In *Why Did I Get Married* (2007), Perry's first film without Madea, four couples go on an annual vacation to ask themselves the titular question. Patricia Agnew (Janet Jackson) is an award-winning psychologist who arranges the trip with her husband Gavin (Malik Yoba), a prominent architect. *Why Did I Get Married* is devoid of what filmmaker Nathaniel Dorsky calls "self-symbol": moments that "fail to take advantage of the self-existing magic of

12 CBS, "Tyler Perry's Amazing Journey to the Top."

things."[13] Every object, location and piece of dialogue in Perry's film is used metaphorically.

Dianne Brock (Sharon Leal) is a lawyer who can't turn off her Blackberry. She brings her laptop on vacation and is shown talking to her secretary in multiple scenes. We understand this to mean that she is too preoccupied with work to spend time with her husband, and therefore family/child. Later in the film her fertility is called into question, along with her desire for motherhood. Marcus (Michael Jai White) is the beefy husband of hair care entrepreneur Angela (Tasha Smith). Marcus was a football player who could have gone pro, but had to stop playing when he was injured. He now works for Angela's company and she emasculates him because he depends on her for money. Marcus and Angela reinforce a narrow perspective regarding the types of success that are available to the Black underclass. In the scenes featuring Angela, Perry took every opportunity available to make a "you can take the girl out of the ghetto" joke. She is shown being loud and aggressive on the train, in upscale retail stores and at her work. White people ridicule Angela for her behavior and it's implied that this is the ultimate punishment. *Why Did I Get Married* gives Perry a platform to confirm his own worldview—a point of view that reinforces strict binaries of man/woman, rich/poor and love/hate.

13 Dorsky, *Devotional Cinema*, 38.

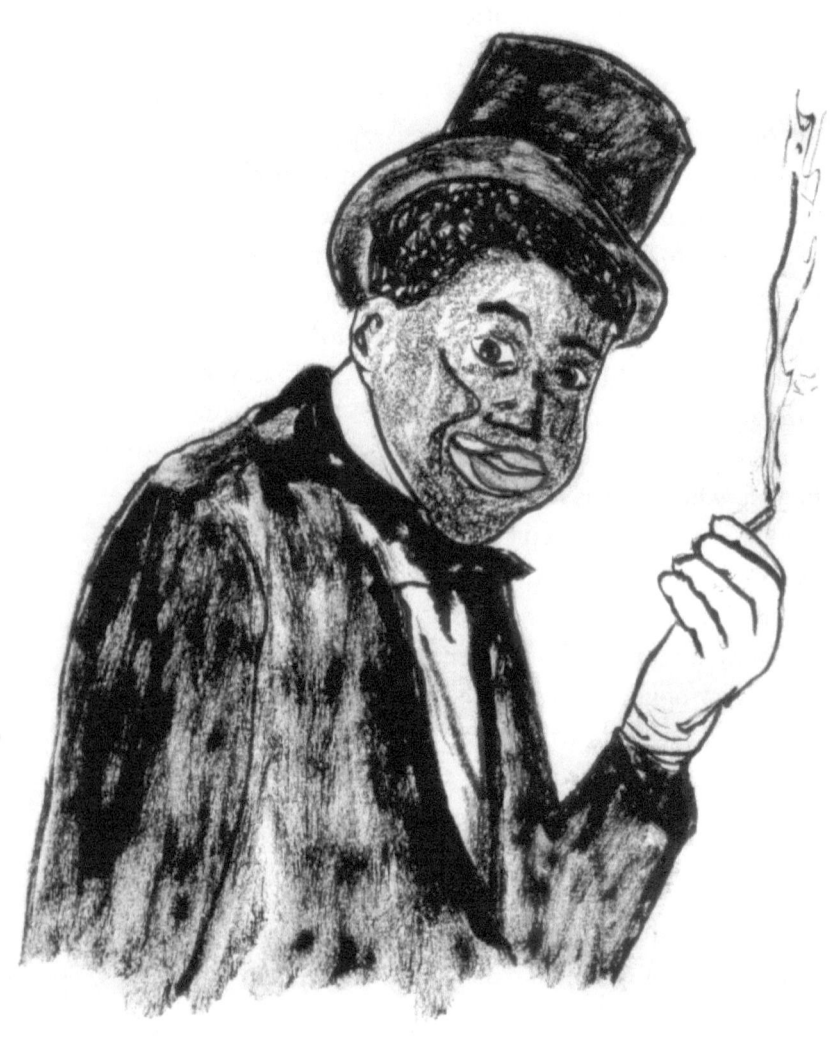

Bert Williams was described by fellow vaudevillian W.C. Fields as "the funniest man I ever saw—and the saddest man I ever knew"

3. Why We Laugh

The minstrel show evolved from vaudeville theater, and featured White actors performing with darkened skin, reddened lips and exaggerated mannerisms. Black actors also donned Blackface for the minstrel show and transformed themselves into the many variants of the slave archetype, including "Toms, Coons, Mulattoes, Mammies, and Bucks," as film historian Donald Bogle succinctly describes them.[14] The legacy of the minstrel show has left a burnt-cork stain on Black comedic performances.

Black actors like Bert Williams could have easily skipped the makeup and simply adopted the lazy smile of Rastus, the pious drawl of Old Uncle Ned or the overblown swagger of Zip Coon, but Blackface has nothing to do with being Black. A Black or Blackface presence is used in cinema to demarcate Whiteness by misrepresenting and dismissing Black culture, creating an oppositional relationship between the races. As James Snead puts it, "[the Negro is] the major figure in which these power relationships of master/slave, civilized/primitive, enlightened/backwards, good/evil, have been embodied in the American subconscious."[15]

14 Bogle, *Toms, Coons, Mulattoes, Mammies, and Bucks.*
15 *Representing Blackness*, 26.

Instead of dedicating time to exposition, mainstream comedic films count on stereotypes to fill in narrative blanks. Comedy relies on opposites and the pairing of Black/White makes for countless visual and cultural jokes. Black-themed comedies use incongruence as a metaphor for the spatial and social realities of Black American life.

Comedian Keith Johnstone teaches that audiences want to watch the situations that they wouldn't want to be involved in. He encourages actors to go for big laughs by staging the fears of their audience. Miscegenation gets this treatment in *Guess Who* (2005), a comedic film about a White man going to meet the family of his Black fiancé for the first time. *Guess Who*, starring Bernie Mac and Ashton Kutcher, resurrects the "crossover-aimed," biracial buddy formula popularized in the eighties by Richard Pryor and Eddie Murphy.[16] The movie is a reference to the 1967 dramatic film *Guess Who's Coming to Dinner*, starring Sidney Poitier and Spencer Tracy, making it a meta-cultural gag.

My favorite scene in Robert Townsend's *Hollywood Shuffle* is the Black Acting School segment. The sketch begins with a group of slaves escaping from the South to the "Promised Land," Minnesota. It's a roll call of archetypes, with Mandingo, the tragic mulatto, the pickaninny and a dimwitted butler played by Townsend. A director stops the scene and Townsend adopts a British accent, explaining that he had to learn to play a slave and "now you can too." At the Black Acting School we see White teachers showing students how to speak jive and "walk like a Black man."

16 Guerrero, *Framing Blackness*, 133.

20

The Black Acting School segment is poignant because of the way that it foreshadows the popularity of hip hop culture, a phenomenon that effectively taught the world how to walk and talk like Black men. In the nineties, hip hop became a useful metonym for representing Blackness within popular culture. Ice Cube, a rapper who came to prominence with the group N.W.A., was able to capitalize on this sea change by starring in and producing a number of Black-themed comedic film franchises, including *Friday* (1995) and *Barbershop* (2002).

Friday was a hood comedy, and like many of its dramatic counterparts, the film is set in the Black metropolis of South Los Angeles. This setting locates *Friday* "in a particular urban history which acknowledges the effects of migration and ghettoization," as scholar Paula J. Massood has researched.[17] The movie follows Craig and Smokey through their neighborhood as they attempt to raise the $200 they owe to local drug dealer Big Worm. Although the jokes are often tasteless, with appearances from Chris Tucker as the perma-fried Smokey, John Witherspoon as Craig's father, Bernie Mac as the adulterous Pastor Clever and AJ Johnson as the desperate crackhead Ezal, it's hard not to laugh during the film. The multi-million dollar success of the movie allowed writer/producer Ice Cube and director F. Gary Gray to continue making films within the studio system.

Barbershop explores the public sphere of a neighborhood barbershop. The series takes place on the South Side of Chicago, another historically significant area for Black

17 Massood, "Which Way to the Promised Land?"

America. In addition to comedians Cedric the Entertainer and Anthony Anderson, Eve—the Ruff Ryders' First Lady—joined the ensemble cast for her first screen role. *Barbershop* has roughly the same plot as *Friday*, but its PG-13 rating prompted a few family-friendly changes. On a cold Saturday in Chicago, Calvin Palmer (Ice Cube) sells his late father's struggling barbershop to greedy loan shark Lester Wallace (Keith David). When Calvin announces the news to his employees, he realizes how important the shop is to the community and attempts to buy it back.

These comedies use several cinematic devices to express a DuBoisian double-consciousness. As I noted before, the movies are set in historically Black areas, virtual cities within cities. The boundaries of these "Black metropolises" become part of the narrative in *Next Friday* (2000) and *Barbershop 2* (2004). In *Next Friday*, Craig moves to the suburb of Rancho Cucamonga to live with his uncle. Through voice-over and dialogue the film compares suburban life to that of the inner city. The punch line of the film is that the suburbs have plenty of their own dangers: ex-girlfriends, neighbors, bosses. *Barbershop 2* addresses the effect of gentrification on the barbershop, and the community at large, when a competing chain called Nappy Cutz opens next door.

Using the temporal constraint of the single day, the Friday and Barbershop series' quickly tour us through the ecosystem of a specific type of urban Black community. While pastors, barbers, city employees, drug dealers and addicts are part of this popularly accepted vision of Black American life, these characters are also rooted in particular historical moments. In Friday, Felicia and Ezal go for easy laughs as the neighborhood crackheads, but their presence in the film is recognition of the crack epidemic that hit South Los Angeles in the late eighties.

In the early aughts, a sub-subgenre known as 'buppie' cinema emerged for those of us, like myself, who only visited the hood to pop in on our less fortunate relatives. Buppie cinema took romantic comedy and swapped the usual suspects for taller, darker and more handsome replacements. I map the territory of the buppie film by the filmographies of four actors: Morris Chestnut, Taye Diggs, Sanaa Lathan and Gabrielle Union. Between the four of them, they've made at least twenty-four Black-themed romantic comedies. While three of four starred in Malcolm Lee's *The Best Man* (1999), this quartet has never shared the silver screen.

Their collective oeuvre concentrates on the lives of upwardly mobile Black professionals. The characters in these films are doctors, lawyers, investment-bankers and other high-income earners who are looking for love and happiness. Buppie films occupy the same space that *The Cosby Show* did in the eighties. We want to see Black people drive around in BMWs and eat at posh restaurants because it looks like progress. It's not that there aren't affluent Blacks—there are, but they typically exist in isolation. It's rare to walk into a courtroom and find that the prosecution, the defense, the judge and the bailiff are all Black, which is what happens in one scene from *The Brothers* (2001).

Buppie films engage the past of the Black middle class in their storylines. Casual mentions of prominent fraternities and sororities, like Alpha Phi Alpha or Delta Sigma Theta, tie characters to historically black colleges and universities. A few films include oblique references to the upper crust social organizations Jack and Jill, and The Links. Even though the characters in buppie movies may vacation in Oak Bluff, Massachusetts, they live in the same neighborhoods as those in the hood films because of restrictive housing practices that have plagued urban African-American populations. Buppie films don't simply document or represent their subjects; instead, like hood films, they actively create a vision that reflects a profound understanding of African-American life. Black-themed comedies operate on two levels to create a lingua franca for Black audiences.

4. Beautiful Dark Twisted Fantasy

Which came first, the rap single or the hood film?

The Fatback Band's 1979 song "King Tim III (Personality Jock)" is widely considered the first rap track, but it was the b-side of a disco record and failed to reach a wide audience. A few weeks later, Sugar Hill Gang released "Rapper's Delight" and introduced the world to hip hop. The hood film predates hip hop by a good ten years. Melvin Van Peebles' raunchy action film *Sweet Sweetback's Baadasssss Song* (1971) is often credited with kicking off the so-called "Blaxploitation" era, but the 1970 flick *Cotton Comes to Harlem* set the tone for the ghetto film.

Cotton was co-written and directed by the late civil rights activist and actor Ossie Davis. The film is an adaptation of Chester Himes' 1965 crime novel of the same name. In the movie, detectives Coffin Ed Johnson (Raymond St. Jacques) and Gravedigger Jones (Godfrey Cambridge) try to recover $87,000 that was swindled from "poor Black folks" by Rev. Deke O'Malley (Calvin Lockhart) in a back-to-Africa hoax. *Cotton* established a lasting cinematic style for Hollywood action/crime movies set in the Black city. Lengthy sequences that highlight Harlem landmarks served as points of identification for Black viewers, and gave Whites a voyeuristic journey through the ghetto. To convey realism, the characters wear current fashions and speak slang. Wide shots followed by close-ups of the various characters indicate a connection between them that is emphasized by the combined use of diegetic and extra-diegetic music. All of the elements in the film work as one to say, "we're all in this (ghetto) together."

Until the 1960s, American Blacks were subject to the legal doctrine of "separate but equal" that supported segregation under the circumstances that both Blacks and Whites had identical facilities, although that condition was rarely enforced. As White flight to the suburbs in the wake of desegregation left cities to decay, Black populations in these areas became more isolated. "Black" became synonymous with "urban."

Hip hop and action films emerged in the seventies to document the urban experience, as jazz and literature had previously done. As these corresponding practices evolved, they began to inform each other and create a new vocabulary for Black male fantasy. "[Blaxploitation movies were] the first time Black kids saw ourselves up on the screen, and we weren't getting our asses kicked; we finally got to kick someone's ass," rapper Ice-T recounts.[18] Black action heroes also got to have lots of sex. They were nothing like the desexualized, well-mannered, bourgeois leading men played by Bill Cosby and Sidney Poitier in the fifties and sixties.

Much has been written about the influence of producer/writer/director/actor Melvin Van Peebles, the

18 "Ice-T's Rap on Blaxploitation - GetBack."

self-proclaimed "James Brown of filmmaking."[19] Peebles
has done everything in his power to encourage the hagiog-
raphy with a series of provocative, apocryphal stories about
working with an impossibly low budget, directing an all-
amateur cast and contracting gonorrhea while doing "stunts"
(and getting workers' comp for it to boot). Grossing more
than ten million dollars, his radical film *Sweet Sweetback's
Baadasssss Song* showed the film industry that a Black
movie could make money. *Sweetback* stars Peebles as a sex
worker, nicknamed Sweetback, who beats two cops to save
a young revolutionary named Mu-Mu. The film chronicles
Sweetback's fugitive journey through Black megapolises,
circus-like brothels and underground gambling parlors,
while providing a critical commentary on the implications
of racism for modern society.

The highest grossing and most referenced Black film of the
seventies is *The Mack* (1973). Max Julien stars as Goldie,
a lost young man who becomes a successful pimp after
he is released from the state penitentiary. *The Mack* was
shot on location and uses the neighborhood thugs to construct its mise en scéne. The film couldn't have happened
without Frank Ward and the Ward brothers, a gang of
pimps who provided the production with money, protec-
tion and access to Oakland's underworld. At its core, *The
Mack* is an attempt to empower its disenfranchised (male)
audience, even at the expense of Black women, who are
characterized as either mothers or ho's. In one dramatic
scene, Goldie's brother Olinga accuses him of teaching
kids to exploit their own kind, to which Goldie responds,
"Well, it's not sick man. It's sick when you have a chance to

19 Moon, *Reel Black Talk*, 343.

get out of a rat-infested ghetto and you don't!" This scene is set to Willie Hutch's classic, and oft-sampled, track "Brother's Gonna Work It Out." The film's most conflicted message has been disseminated through a number of popular rap songs.

Even dialogue from The Mack has found its way into popular rap. There's "Stay Fly" by Three 6 Mafia, Dr. Dre's "Rat-Tat-Tat-Tat," "Rap's A Hustla" from Cormega, Mobb Deep's "Still Shinin,'" "Pimpin Part 2" by 50 Cent, and others. It would be impossible to count the number of songs that were inspired by *The Mack*, and even more difficult to track the rappers whose public personae were influenced by the film. In the making-of documentary *Mackin' Ain't Easy* (2002), Dr. Todd Boyd explains that rappers liken themselves to the pimp because they see him as an intellectual. "Any man can control a woman's body; a great pimp controls their minds," the blind man tells Goldie in the *The Mack*. The pimp is valued for how well he "spits game," and so is the rapper.

If a rapper doesn't identify with a pimp or needs a tougher image, he (or, rarely, she) will take on the persona of the drug dealer. Although the drug dealer has a place in marginalized Black communities, the fictionalized account that is broadcast by rappers is often a stylized imitation of Tony Montana (Al Pacino), from the 1983 Brian De Palma film *Scarface*. *Scarface* is not a race film, but it does promote a rags-to-riches story of uplift that Black audiences identify with.

In contrast to dramatic films, the uplift ideology in action films begins with material progress and ends with death or moral redemption. The purpose of life for these protagonists is to *Get Rich Or Die Trying*, as the title of 50 Cent's 2005 autobiographical film states. Like *The Mack*, *Scarface* shows the accumulation of wealth as the only effective way out of poverty.

Mario Van Peebles' directorial debut, *New Jack City* (1991) is the prototypical Black gangster movie of the 1990s. Nino Brown (Wesley Snipes), the film's main character, has been de-fictionalized into an urban folk hero. Nino Brown, of course, idolizes Tony Montana. The movie starts with Queen Latifah's explosive cover of "Living for the City" while a crane shot of New York City celebrates the metropolis in all of its pre-9/11 grandeur. *New Jack City* is set in Harlem during the crack era and blasts the new music of the streets from beginning to end.

Nino Brown is the Machiavellian leader of the drug gang "Cash Money Brothers." The CMB take over a housing project to "centralize operations," and their impact begins to tyrannize the neighborhood. Mario van Peebles, Judd Nelson, and Ice-T star as cops trying to take Nino down. *New Jack City* is visibly influenced by the Black action films of the seventies, and makes a conscious effort to reinvent the form for a younger generation.

In the film the lifestyle of the drug dealers is cool. They go to dance clubs where Flava Flav is deejaying, and Fab5Freddy plays a few songs. Keith Sweat sings in their backyard. The dealers refer to killing people as "singing a lullaby." Art Sims, creative director/founder of 11:24 Design Agency created the posters for *New Jack City*. He told the American Institute of Graphic Arts "Wesley Snipes was the drug dealer—the bad guy—but I wanted to show him on the poster, smoking a cigarette and wearing sunglasses."[20] Even though Nino gets his in the end, he is a much more appealing character than the comical Afrocentrism of Ice-T's good guy, Scotty Appleton. Lil Wayne, a rapper currently at the height of his career, named his concert film *The Story of Nino Brown*. When was the last time anything was named after Scotty Appleton?

While *New Jack City* recounts the glamorous drug trade in New York, *Boyz N The Hood* (1991) presents a stylized look at the banal violence of South Central Los Angeles. *Boyz* subverts the conventional coming-of-age story to explore contemporary segregation. We're introduced to Tre Styles (Cuba Gooding Jr.), Ricky Baker (Morris Chestnut) and Doughboy (Ice Cube) as preteens. After getting into a fight at school Tre is sent to live with his father, Furious, a stern disciplinarian, so that he can learn to be a man. Ricky and Doughboy are Tre's neighbors. They are raised by their mother Brenda (Tyra Ferrell), a semi-abusive woman who openly prefers Ricky over Doughboy. As children, the boys traverse their neighborhood for dead bodies and are subjected to insults and attacks from older kids. As young adults, they look for honeys/bitches/women/pussy and watch out for drive-bys or cops. They are helpless to the brutality that afflicts their community.

20 Willis, "Art Sims."

Although I characterize *Boyz* as an action film, it is also a drama in the tradition of Micheaux. Through the voice of Furious Styles, *Boyz* teaches its presumably male audience about gentrification, safe sex and manhood. The audience learns what Tre learns. *Boyz* is heavy with consciousness, a serious film with serious actors. The story feels authentic because of its rap soundtrack, fashionable costumes and repeated use of words like "nigga" and "motherfucker." I'm willing to believe that *Boyz* speaks to a reality, even if it is not my own.

Furious Styles teaches the Boyz how II be men

In *Boyz*, Ricky dies before he can accept his football scholarship to USC and Tre ends up at Morehouse. Doughboy doesn't go to school, but he wasn't a criminal. *Menace II Society* (1993), the Hughes brothers' first major effort, follows the boys that *Boyz* glosses over, the nihilists. *Menace* is set in Watts and told through the voiceover narration of Caine (Tyrin Turner), a young drug dealer. The film takes place during the summer following Caine's high school graduation and begins with a shockingly casual shooting of two Korean shop owners by O-Dog (Larenz Tate), Caine's best friend.

Caine's father was a drug dealer and his mother was a junkie. In a flashback scene we see him witness a murder and learn how to hold a gun as a child. Caine is a typical teenage boy with a gun. He deals drugs, steals cars and kills people. He lives with his grandparents and listens begrudgingly to his grandfather's admonishments. In the narration, Caine considers his mortality. In contrast, O-Dog has no family and no conscience. He has no foresight or hindsight. As Caine explains in the beginning of the film, "O-Dog was the craziest nigga alive. America's nightmare. Young, Black and didn't give a fuck."

While *Menace* is stylistically related to earlier Black action films, its message is convoluted by sensationalism. The role of O-Dog allowed the filmmakers to kill any other character without reason. O-Dog was a way for audiences to imagine murder without consequence. Caine attempts to redeem himself, but he still dies, while O-Dog gets away with it all. This type of tourism is more problematic than the simulated flaneury of the camera.

Los Angeles connects *Boyz N The Hood* and *Menace II Society*. As a native of the sprawling city, I understand how mobility underscored my existence there. There was life before my driver's license and after it. The young men in these films can leave, they have cars and driver's licenses, but they are trapped nonetheless. They are defined by their skin, their neighborhood and their peers. In both films, a young Black man dies at the hands of another, confirming the same myth that the directors claim to destroy. *Boyz* and *Menace* gave America an updated image of the ghetto. "I've been a menace to society since *Menace II Society*," intones T.I. in the beginning of his song "King of da South." Rappers use these films as fodder for shorthand descriptions of their disadvantaged youths.

While popular rap in the early nineties was "gritty," "raw" and straight out of Compton/Brooklyn, by the middle of the decade the focus had shifted to ostentatiousness. Hype Williams, a young filmmaker from New York, emerged as a prolific director of music videos. Williams' works were imaginative and ambitious. His shorts provided a cinematic expression of hip hop culture that was otherwise absent from television and movies. Williams' music videos presented contemporary Black men and women in an opulent, neo-Baroque world, similar to the works of painter Kehinde Wiley.

In *Belly* (1998), William's first feature film, he takes on the Black action genre. *Belly* follows Tommy 'Buns' Bundy (DMX) and Sincere (Nas), small time drug dealers who want more from life. After a bout of theft and murder, these petty thugs have spiritual awakenings. Buns is convinced by a Farrakhan-esque character to devote himself to the race, and Tommy moves to Africa. I'm interested in *Belly* as an extended music video. Aside from irrelevant subplots featuring cameos from hip hop celebrities, *Belly* doesn't stray far from its antecedents. *Belly* is an abbreviation of the movies I've previously discussed. It's like watching those films on fast-forward. All substance is lost and the intensity of the film is derived from its fast pace, saturated color, exaggerated visual compositions and intense soundtrack. It's a race film for the MTV generation.

5. Repeated Listening

From the start of this essay, you knew that I was Black and female, but maybe you guessed that I was also middle-class and college-educated. Likely I have the same stories as other Black girls who grew up in first-ring suburbs. Their parents also listened to what I disdainfully call "smooth jazz," and what writer Britt Julious respectfully calls "Quiet Storm."[1] Luther, Sade, Vanessa Wiliams, Anita Baker, Babyface, late-career Stevie, and so on. I knew this monotonous Black music from morning commutes and other long drives. I associate it with carsickness. Motown still existed, but I was more familiar with it from my favorite biopic, *The Jacksons: An American Dream* (1992). I haven't thought about it until now, but I didn't grow up listening to hip hop. It replaced soul music in the Black community at a pivotal point, but I missed out. I was raised Christian and my parents kept it out of the house. My childhood sounded like 94.7 The Wave, "Southern California's place to relax … and unwind." What happens in those ellipses, I'm unsure. The Wave was a radio station that pioneered the "new adult contemporary format" with a mix of jazz-inspired pop vocalists and instrumentals.

I still like that kind of music, or at least it's what I listen to when I'm by myself. Sure, it's "bad," but I'm willing to

1 Julius, "In Which You're Listening to the Quiet Storm."

bet money that those who share my demographic profile have a soft spot for entertainers like Whitney Houston that can't be explained. Whitney, as I call her, is the perfect analogy for Black cultural production. Her career exists at the intersection of many distribution points and she tightrope walks the color line with such grace. Like many components of Black culture, Whitney Houston came from the church. Her mother, Cissy, was a prominent gospel singer and Whitney sang in the choir. Initially working as a fashion model, Whitney was one of the first women of color to be on the cover of Seventeen Magazine.

In 1985, Whitney signed with Arista for a Guinness World Record-breaking tenure as the first female to debut an album at number one, the first with seven consecutive number one hits and the only artist with seven back-to-back multiplatinum albums. Whitney is also recognized for integrating MTV. Before her and Michael Jackson, the channel was all White. And like Michael Jackson, Whitney's career is epitomized by her audience's so-called colorblindness. For twenty years, writers and interviewers have liked to pretend that Whitney is America's princess, not Black America's princess. The media usually has the opposite reaction to Black talent.

While she has only performed in four films, Whitney has appeared on the soundtrack of almost forty. The soundtrack album is a strange artifact. The music is inextricably tied to an image. This is the part when _____. When I put on any other record, I fill in the visual blanks. Or, more likely, I pretend I'm in a movie. In film school I was discouraged from using popular music in my work because the viewer would already have a strong association with the song, especially if the song had already played in a movie. It was too easy to make a scene more meaningful because of someone else's work. In an original motion picture soundtrack album, the scene is absent, but the music is made more powerful by the memory of image.

Whitney's debut screen performance as Rachel Marron in *The Bodyguard* (1992) actively interrogates the diegesis of the film. Her participation on the soundtrack album further confounds the narrative of the film with that of her own career. In the movie Whitney plays a music superstar who is being sent death threats by a stalker. Former Secret Service agent Frank Farmer (Kevin Costner) is hired to protect her. When I was a child my parents didn't let me see *The Bodyguard*, but I understood it deeply—as a result of repeated listening to the soundtrack. The songs on *The Bodyguard* soundtrack are the hits of Rachel Marron in the movie, but the album achieved incredible commercial success for Whitney in real life. The soundtrack was certified platinum seventeen times, and took home the Album of the Year honors at the 1994 Grammy Awards. Whitney Houston's performance of "I Will Always Love You" has become a part of American cultural history; I'd guess that most people don't even know it from *The Bodyguard*. Instead, it seems to have always been and to forever endure in our collective imaginations. My favorite song on the album was "Run To You." I would push play on my stereo and sing it emphatically to my younger sister, with whom I shared a room. This happened at least once a day for about a year. I'm still transported when I hear the first few synthesized notes of the ballad.

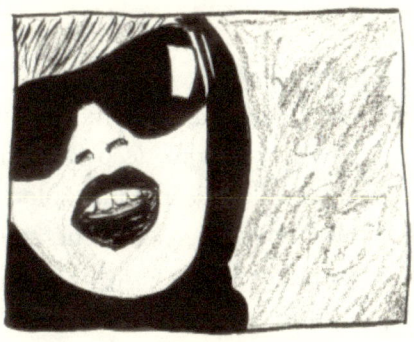

Not Gon' Cry is my jam

The scatting of Whitney's "Exhale" is also permanently fixed in my memory. The song is track one on the *Waiting to Exhale* soundtrack, an album that was on heavy rotation in my mother's Dodge Caravan. I preferred the four and a half minute Mary J. Blige opus "Not Gon' Cry." As a third-grader I sang the entirety of "Not Gon' Cry" in concert with thirty other students in an impromptu lunchtime rendition. "Not Gon' Cry" is a battle song for Black women. The song is anthemic and its validation of Black vernacular English is empowering. In contrast to the film's flat translation of Terri McMillan's best-selling novel, the soundtrack functions as a compelling document of Black female cultural production. The *Waiting to Exhale* soundtrack went seven times platinum and stayed at the top of the Billboard charts for five weeks. Whitney's hit song took home a Grammy for Best R&B Song in 1997, two years after the film's initial release. Despite the record's pop feminist conceits, a man's name—Kenneth 'Babyface' Edmonds—is emblazoned on every track. Babyface's credits include producer, writer, composer, reducing the women to "mere" performers. But his performance on "All Night Long" is the weakest, and I'm not just saying that.

Whitney hasn't returned to the big screen since her starring role in *The Preacher's Wife* (1996). The film is about
an urban pastor who prays for help and receives it in the
form of an angel who wants to sleep with his wife. *The
Preacher's Wife* was slated to be a holiday blockbuster, but
it fared poorly at the box office. What's notable about this
film is that the soundtrack is a gospel album performed
exclusively by Whitney. Consequently, the soundtrack
was multiplatinum and is the best-selling gospel album
of all time. I probably went to see *The Preacher's Wife* at
the movie theater, but I can't remember. I know we had
the soundtrack, but it was my parents' and I didn't bother
to listen to it. I didn't care for gospel music, unless it was
from *Sister Act 2*.

Sister Act 2: Back in the Habit (1993) introduced a younger
generation to gospel music and paved the way for acts like
Kirk Franklin & The Family. I had a babysitter who was
obsessed with the 'Oh Happy Day' sequence in the film.
Her name was Shanice. She had long dookie braids, hoop
earrings and a big keloid on the back of her left ear. The
scene features a montage of the choir practicing the hymn
"Oh Happy Day" and culminates in a school assembly
where the young militant, Ahmal James (Ryan Toby), suc-
cessfully uses the whistle register. Shanice would rewind
the tape and watch the high note over and over again.
Lauryn Hill also appears in *Sister Act 2* and her expressive voice can be heard on the soundtrack as well. Lauryn
played Rita Watson, a steel-eyed would-be singer discouraged by her single mother's admonishments. Sheryl Lee
Ralph played Rita's mother with an unconvincing West
Indian accent. Whenever appropriate, my brother's would

repeat her best line to me in their own West Indian accents. "There are a lot of talented people right down there on the streets singing their 'shoulda-coulda-woulda's'" Some time later in college, I was talking about *Sister Act 2* with a friend, a Black girl, and I pulled out my iPod to play a song from the soundtrack. My friend stopped me and asked incredulously "How come every Black person I know has the *Sister Act 2* soundtrack on their iPod?!" and we laughed because it was true.

6. What Are You Looking At

I asked my (White) boyfriend what makes him think that something is Black. "What is it that says to you 'This isn't for me?'" I asked. I wanted to ask other people too, but it's a difficult conversation to have and most people aren't up to the challenge. It's hard to acknowledge our own prejudice. No one wants to think of him or herself as racist. So I talked to my boyfriend. After talking for an hour, we figured it out. Whereas I ask, "How do I know what I know," he thinks, "I don't know what I don't know." Anything that is immediately unfamiliar is read as Other, and the default Other in America is Black.

My anecdotes belie my demographics, and my demographics influence my purchasing decisions. The economic engine of most cultural distribution, and therefore consumption, is advertising. Radio has spots, television has commercials and motion picture advertising includes both those methods and more. I can tell when a movie is being marketed to a Black audience. They turn up the music (rap, soul or gospel, depending), parade their colored stars and throw something Black in there (guns, dancing or church, depending).

In 2007, the average marketing budget for a major theatrical release was thirty-five million dollars.[2] My favorite method of movie marketing is the press junket. Although I've never experienced it directly, my understanding is that writers are given an all-expenses paid trip to an exotic locale to watch a movie and interview the cast. Anytime an actor is shown talking about her film while seated in front of a large movie banner, it's probably at a press junket. I'm fascinated by the effort it takes to construct a gulf between the film's narrative and the world "behind-the-scenes." It seems at odds with the enormous measures taken to assert the authenticity of the film. I'm interested in the contradictions and commonalities between representation and reality.

The concept of Blackness is further confused by an overall discord between biology and culture. Is a movie Black because the cast is Black, or because the crew is Black? This ideology is called biological essentialism. It offers that one's intrinsic nature is determined by her biology. I am Black because I am Black. For a long time I refused to "act Black" because I didn't feel comfortable with its definition. I'm sure I wasn't the only kid who was accused of "acting White." A cultural definition of Blackness says I am Black because I act Black, but how do we define a Black performance?

Even cartoon characters can be read as Black. Skeeter from Nickelodeon's *Doug* was the only kid to rap and break dance in the fictional Bluffington. Flight School, a

2 Joshi, "Movie Advertising and the Stock Market Valuation of Studios: A Case of 'Great Expectations'?"

41

web based t-shirt company has a shirt proclaiming in bold letters "Skeeter was Black." The rendering of Blackness in popular culture reads a bit like Wikipedia's "List of African-American Stereotypes." The list characterizes Blackness by attributes such as profanity, violence, crime, athletic ability and poverty. I'd add skin color, hair, sexuality, extended family, spirituality, food, musical aptitude, rhythm and style. These are the primary indicators used to depict Blackness in moving images, with varying degrees of distinction. Perhaps an "authentic" race film knowingly, willingly verifies and contradicts these guidelines.

The key visual signifiers of ethnicity in life, as in film, are skin and hair. During the worst part of the winter, I walk around Chicago with my hood up and no skin showing but my eyes. I sometimes wonder if the people behind me know that I'm Black. Maybe they can tell from my hips, I think. The freezing cold offers a momentary disruption of race. While I move from place to place, I'm just another adult in a ski mask. Most other days, I fail the paper bag test. My skin is a darker brown with red undertones. I would have worked in the fields, closer to the house than farther away from it. My hair is type 4a. I have fragile, tightly coiled strands that are densely packed on my head. When I sleep my hair gets mashed into a ½ inch thick Afro, which I comb out to three or four inches. If my hair is pulled taut it nearly reaches my shoulders.

In 2009, comedians Chris Rock and Jeff Stilson teamed up to make *Good Hair*, a documentary chronicling the relationship between Black women and their hair. The film humorously demystifies concepts like "creamy crack" (chemical straighteners) and "White girl flow" (hair that blows in the wind) for a White audience. While the women in the film detail what they do to their hair, Rock never asks them *why*. Despite Reverend Al Sharpton's rhetoric about wearing our "economic oppression on our heads," *Good Hair* is noticeably apolitical. In his interviews, Rock begins to expose the implicit dialogue between Blacks and their stylists, but gets cold feet, preferring to lighten the mood with one-liners. He calls this non-judgmental. I call it non-committal. Nonetheless, it was Hollywood's first feature devoted to Black hair. Our hair care contributes to a multi-billion dollar industry that is propelled by fashioning race.

I'm suspicious of movies that ignore the politics of style. I call foul when I see a Black woman going to sleep without wearing a silk scarf. Few films delve into this subject. For *School Daze* (1988) Spike Lee went *West Side Story* (1961) in his fanciful fight between the dark-skinned, nappy headed Jiggaboos and their high-yellow counterparts, the Wannabes. The women fight-dance in a hair salon called Madame Re-Re's. In *Something New* (2006) Kenya McQueen (Sanaa Lathan) is a successful corporate exec who has chosen a career over romance. She develops a flirtation with her landscaper Brian, "a White boy," who slowly brings her out of her shell. Early in their relation-ship they're on a hike when it starts to rain and Kenya swears and darts under a tree. When her date asks what's wrong she yells "My hair!" Brian draws the line when Kenya stops him from touching her hair during lovemak-ing. After they break up, Kenya starts wearing her hair "natural." The movie ends with Brian running his hands through her luscious coils.

There's a running gag in the Black community that says to never, ever touch a women's hair. The joke is that you'll run across a weave track, or a mousetrap, or god knows what. NPR contributor Allison Keyes wrote a piece outlining why you should "think twice before you palm someone's puff."[3] Keyes spoke specifically about strangers who wanted to pet her Afro and garnered flack from commenters for calling it a race issue. Anticipating this reaction Keyes noted, "Let's have a reality check here. For hundreds of years, Whites had permission to do anything they wanted to Black people, and that includes things far worse than touching our hair." In filmmaking, hairstyling is used in conjunction with costuming to flesh out an underdeveloped character, or provide a cultural context for a major one. In his essay 'Black Hair/Style Politics' cultural theorist Kobena Mercer demands "a critical analysis of the multi-faceted economy of black hair as a condition for appropriate aesthetic judgments."[4]

He also argues "There are no just black hair-styles, just black hair-styles."[5] With that in mind I want us to remember the hairstyles and costumes of Robert Townsend's 1997 comedic romp *B*A*P*S*. The movie stars Halle Berry and Natalie Desselle as Nisi and Mickey, a pair from Decatur, Georgia who go to Hollywood to become video vixens. On their journey Nisi is hired to pretend to be the granddaughter of a White millionaire's long lost love. In return he teaches them how to live as Black American Princesses.

3 Keyes, "Keep Your Hands Off The Hair."

4 Mercer, "Black Hair/Style Politics," 20.

5 Ibid., 21.

B*A*P*S traffics in exaggerations. Nisi and Mickey are decked out in the most outrageous fashions of the Black ghetto. Ruth E. Carter, the Oscar-nominated costume designer, must have worked overtime on this film. Nisi wears a platinum blond braided crown, a skin-tight neon colored bodysuit, gold fronts and ridiculously long fake nails. Roger Ebert found the message of the movie to be "that two homegirls can find wealth and happiness if only they wear blond wigs, get rid of those gold teeth and country vocabularies, and are nice to rich old white men." [6]

B*A*P*S reminds me of *Act Da Fool*, the 2010 short by famed filmmaker Harmony Korine that was commissioned by the fashion label Proenza Schouler. Both of these films link Black women to the ghetto, not by location but through fashion. *Act Da Fool* fetishizes the bodies of working class Black women by outfitting them in couture as they gallivant around abandoned lots drinking 40s, smoking weed and even playing basketball. A girl with a southern dialect who swears intently and describes herself and her friends as "wild animals" narrates the film. The Proenza Schouler website features interviews with Korine and designers Jack McCollough and Lazaro Hernandez discussing the film. Korine says he found his actresses by asking around for the "the greatest living delinquents." [7] Hernandez says that Korine is "trying to find beauty in what society has refused." [8] *Act Da Fool* uses Black poverty to sell five hundred dollar paint splattered jeans to White women. The film does what

6 Ebert, "B.A.P.S."

7 "Proenza Schouler."

8 Ibid.

the runway cannot. Scholar K. Wayne Yang asserts that "the ghetto is not where Black people live but rather where Blackness is contained.", The Black city provides a convenient location to tell the story of the underdog in perpetuity.

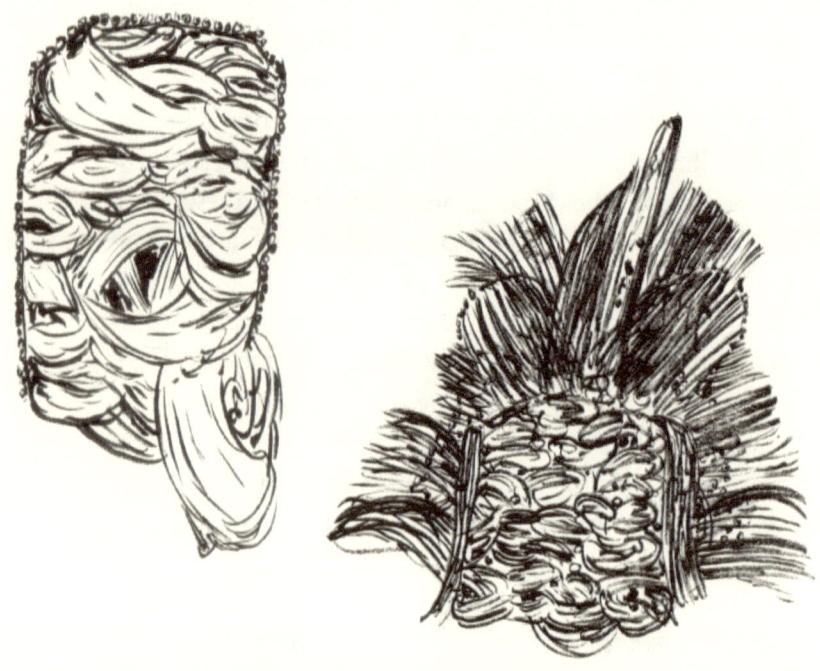

The extreme hairstyles of Black American Princesses

9 Paperson, "The Postcolonial Ghetto: Seeing Her Shape and His Hand," 10.

7. The Talking Circle

During Obama's presidential campaign he was charged with using "dog-whistle politics." Obama would include references to Malcolm X, Martin Luther King Jr., and other Black figures. These mentions went largely unnoticed by White audiences, but they were immediately recognizable to Blacks. When appropriate, Obama also used African-American Vernacular English to further signify his Blackness.

In some situations I'm deemed more authentic if I can slip into a blaccent. In others, I'm thought of as dumb. Since I am solidly middle-class, I learned how to code-switch early. I know when to speak perfect English and when to drop a "girl" on the end of my sentence. I might say "don't be movin' my stuff" to my boyfriend if I'm not upset, but I want him to know that I'm serious. I've also been known to let out an "oh lawd" in exasperation. I can't say which words change or how, although there is a very detailed Wikipedia entry on the subject. I can speak both Standard American English and Black Vernacular English fluently. I switch back and forth naturally. I'm also good at speaking both simultaneously when I want to assert my Blackness and deny my connection to another Black at the same— like to that guy on the bus who says, "Damn girl, you lookin' good."

What constitutes a blaccent is made more nebulous by hip hop and its associated slang. Everyone is "hustlin'" every day. Or maybe they're a "hustla'." As linguist John McWhorter notes, "Black English, especially the cadence, is becoming America's youth lingua franca, especially since the mainstreaming of hip hop."[10] Hip hop slang is derived from a number of sources including gangs, prisons and inventive young people. In the same way that hip hop is confused with Blackness, the criminal origins of its slang are conflated with Blackness as well.

Performing Blackness relies on a mastery of the cadence and rhythm of language. This is most clearly visible in the work of performers Anna Deavere Smith and Sarah Jones. While both women have had bit roles in commercial films, they are wildly successful in theater circles. They write and perform minimal, one-woman shows in which they convincingly portray a diverse cast of characters through the use of voice. Smith and Jones are able to transform their voices so dramatically that it sounds as if they are channeling spirits. If you closed your eyes you wouldn't think they were Black. As a result, their Black voices are pitch-perfect. For example, when Jones appeared on Def Poetry Jam she wore long braids and opens with "Wassup New York." She used a distinctly East Coast hip hop cadence for the duration of her piece. Conversely, while presenting at the Aspen Ideas Festival she spoke with straightened hair and no blaccent. Jones works in isolation, which makes it easy to know when she is performing Blackness, but the same cues are visible in mainstream cinema as well.

10 John, "Sounding Black."

In addition to the colloquialisms popularized by young adults, there are also the motivational words that come from the warm, leathery voices of elder Blacks. I'm thinking of Maya Angelou, James Earl Jones or Morgan Freeman. These actors vocalize dignity and respect. Even when they speak sternly, like Freeman's Principal Joe Clark in *Lean On Me* (1989) or Jones in *The Sandlot* (1993), we know they just want us to succeed. Freeman's stately style of communication has led to his repeated casting as the "Magical Negro" in several Hollywood films. He often plays selfless men who possess deep spiritual wisdom. He's also played God twice.

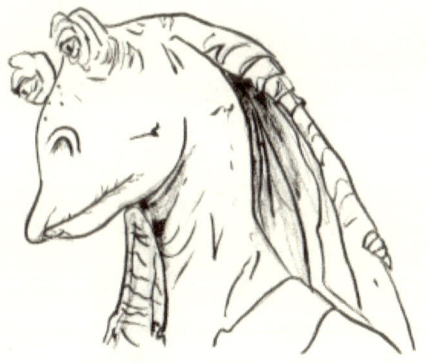

"Why me-sa always da one?"

The most maligned linguistic tradition in Black cinema history is cooning, first popularized by Stepin Fetchit. Fetchit was the stage persona of Lincoln Perry, the first Black movie star. Fetchit was the "laziest man alive," a slow talking, slow moving, slow thinking servant who was known to bulge his eyes with fright at the mention of ghosts. Even those who are not familiar with Fetchit would recognize his legacy in Jar Jar Binks, the clumsy Gungan from *Episode 1: The Phantom Menace* (1999). Jar Jar's speech is heavily influenced by minstrelsy; "Me berry berry scay-yud" and "Why me-sa always da one?" are exceptionally ripe lines. Jar Jar Binks is "a black man in frog face," wrote Patricia Williams in The Nation. She continues, "And whether it were a white man, a black woman or Al Jolson himself beneath the mask, what would still make all the clowning so particularly insulting is the fact that Jar Jar's speech is a weird pidgin mush of West African, Caribbean and African-American linguistic styles."[11]

Comedian and actress Mo'Nique has been asked numerous times why she uses such foul language in her act. In an interview with CNN, she explains, "I come from a family of cussers, baby. Listen, growing up, my aunts and uncles, you would go over their house to play spades and there would be some cussing going on and you'd have to say 'I didn't even know you could put those words together!'"[12]

The first curse word that I learned was "fucker." A bully named Jeremy called me a bitch in kindergarten. I didn't know what to say to him, but I knew I needed to retaliate. I consulted my best friend Molly and she provided me with the f-bomb. The next day during recess I called him a fucker and he stopped messing with me. This was my unofficial introduction to "strategic swearing." The Harvard Business Review devoted an entire episode of IdeaCast to find out if "smart bosses use the f-bomb as a tool."[13] Although their research focuses on the workplace, they developed two types of swearing that I think extend

11 Williams, "Racial Ventriloquism."

12 CNN, "Mo'Nique On Award Nominations."

13 McGinn, "Should Leaders Ever Swear?"

outside professional settings. The first is "social swearing," used informally or "backstage" to create solidarity and the second is "annoyance swearing" used to relieve stress. In response to HBR, scholar Bob Sutton adds that swearing can be used to effectively convey emotional intensity and authenticity.[14] In other words, "there is no way to convey 'fuck you' with polite speech."[15]

Actor Samuel L. Jackson has built a career on strongly worded diatribes that in recent years have evolved to include iPhone apps and videogames. I can't even think of him without the word "motherfucker" popping into my head. Jackson revels in his bad ass image and uses profanity for comedic effect. We all love his jive brother act. My favorite moment of jive in recent history is the dialogue between First Jive Dude (Norman Alexander Gibbs) and Second Jive Dude (Al White) in *Airplane!* (1980). In this classic bit of modern comedy, two Black men converse and pontificate in slang while subtitles translate their words. The first line is "Shi', man, tha' honkey mo'fo' mess wi' my ol' lady, man, I rap tha' dude upside his head, man." This means, "Golly, that white fellow should stay away from my wife or I will punch him." The writers thought of the scene after they saw the movie *Shaft* (1971) and "didn't understand what [the actors] were saying."[16] Before their audition Gibbs and White had rehearsed the scene several times. "We knew what they wanted," White explained in a behind-the-scenes interview, "They wanted jive as a

14 Sutton, "Strategic Use of Swearing in the Workplace."
15 Jay, "The Utility and Ubiquity of Taboo Words."
16 *The Making of Jive Talk from Airplane!*

language. Which it is not. Jive is only a word here, or a phrase there." "We actually created a language," Gibbs added, "In order for it to be consistent we needed to find a key, or a code, so that we would be able to have a sense of rhythm." [17]

I want to consider what the language of film "sounds" like with a blaccent. Without getting too bogged down with semiotics and linguistics, the language of film includes what is visible in the scene (actors, location, costumes), cinematography (point-of-view, movement, scale), editing (sequence, duration, transitions) and sound (diegetic and non-diegetic). As if that isn't enough, the production of a film is also enmeshed in political and economic negotiations involving the studio, cast, crew and audience. Just as there isn't one blaccent in the spoken word, there isn't one blaccent for the screen. If a film isn't Black enough, the studios darken it, and if it's too Black—well, we don't usually get to see those ones.

17 Ibid.

8. A Prothesis

During my freshman year of college I was watching
Richard Pryor's 1982 concert film *Live on the Sunset Strip*
with my friend and his roommate. The roommate was
already looking at the film when I arrived at their dorm
room. I settled in on the couch and became immersed in
the movie. I'd seen it before on Comedy Central, edited
and much less interesting. After indulging us for an hour,
my friend began to pout in the corner. We ignored him
and continued to laugh at Pryor's absurdities. Suddenly
he grabbed the remote, turned the TV off and announced,
"Richard Pryor is only funny to Black people and people
from the South." His dig was profound to me, not
because it was true, but because it was so confrontational.
I quickly became representative of "Black people" and his
roommate "people from the South." My friend felt marginalized, probably for the first time in his life. He was
watching a film that openly discussed performances of
Blackness with two people very unlike himself.

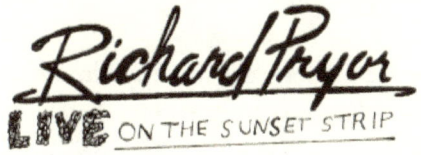

Pryor appeared in over forty films

Another time I saw *Beauty Shop* (2005), the *Barber Shop 2* spin-off starring Queen Latifah, at a theater in Los Angeles. A friend had begged me to go with her. "Have you ever gone to this type of movie?" she wondered, "It's fun. Everyone yells at the screen. You can even throw popcorn." I had been to that type of movie, with that type of audience. I'd spent most of my life avoiding such situations. But I went. My friend had a blast amongst the ringing cell phones, crying babies and general lack of decorum. She enjoyed the cultural tourism and sucked her teeth with the best of them. I was worried about being mistaken for just another Black person.

The film apparatus is an inherently social practice. Production, distribution and exhibition all involve some level of collaboration. As a filmmaker I require a subject. As a distributor I require a seller. As an exhibitor I require an audience. The various negotiations made between these roles create a dynamic experience. As a contemporary spectator I have a range of ways to encounter moving images. I can choose to watch television on-demand or live, with advertising or without. I can watch on a computer through pirated torrents, streaming providers like Netflix, proprietary sites like iTunes, future dollar bins like Hulu or I can still pop in a DVD. If I decide to go to the movie theater I'm presented with the least choice, but the most collective experience.

Surrounding, and often eclipsing the film object is a range of conventions that serve to extend its reach. Trailers, movie posters, press junkets and awards each provide implicit and explicit contexts for the work, as do film length, show time, rating and so on. I'm calling these attributes "exhibition prosthetics," after Joseph Grigely's concept of fine art exhibition practices. In his book on the subject, he asks, "To what extent are these various exhibition conventions actually part of the art—and not merely an extension of it?"[1]

Few film images are able to transcend their site specificity. Viewers approach each cinema encounter with their own set of expectations that create distinct experiences. Those experiences are altered by introducing more people to the spectacle. A Christmas movie is different than a summer blockbuster. Spike Lee's ambitious biopic *Malcolm X* became a source of pride in the Black community because it was resurrected by a group of wealthy, influential Black entertainers after being shelved by its studio. The circumstances surrounding the production and the message of the film were modified by the LA riots that preceded its release. It is difficult to say where a film is actually located.

In Black cinema practices, exhibition prosthetics illuminate the ambiguities of the color line. A film's intended demographics are revealed through advertising, theater selection, budget, studios, directors and actors. In a partnership with AMC, Earvin "Magic" Johnson opened six multiplexes in Black metropolises across the country. StarzinBlack, BET, VH1Soul and virtual ghettos, like UPN in the late nineties, target Black television audiences. Netflix has genres titled "African-American Action," "African-American Drama" and an algorithm to support this disenfranchisement. How do conventional, separate modes of distribution collide with Black imagination?

1 Grigely, *Exhibition Prosthetics*.

9. The Exhibitionists

The first time I noticed the ICE theater in Chatham I was taking the Red Line to get my hair done at the Dudley Beauty School. I saw the yellow letters spelling out C-I-N-E-M-A from the train. I didn't see the building again for four years, but I visited their website often. I liked the name. Inner City Entertainment. It was clear and sticky. ICE was a descriptive acronym that reminded me of my adopted home. Hollywood has stars. Chicago has winter.

It's surprisingly easy to find information about the owners of Inner City Entertainment. They've made themselves completely available to the community. I called the phone number on their website and left a quick message, fully expecting to be ignored or approached by an assistant. Alisa Starks, President of ICE, called me back the next day. I was thrilled. It's doubtful that I will ever meet another Black woman theater owner again.

Our first meeting was botched. I forgot to call and confirm. I was too excited. I got up early to prepare. I should have known something was up when I forgot my wallet and had to go back home after waiting for the bus for fifteen minutes. I listened to podcasts the whole ride down, approximately one hour. I couldn't find the theater. I remembered it being bigger. I didn't remember the strip mall surrounding it. Had that Home Depot always been there?

Eventually I found it and smiled at the big letters. C-I-N-E-M-A they announced. "Cinema," I agreed. I stared at the marquee and imagined someone changing the letters each week. They hadn't replaced it with an LED board and I liked that. I stood at the entrance sort of looking for a movie to watch: *The Warrior's Way, Burlesque, Faster, Tangled, Harry Potter and the Deathly Hallows Part 1, The Next Three Days, Skyline, Unstoppable, For Colored Girls* and *Megamind* were my options. Adult tickets cost $7.00 for a matinee and $9.50 in the evening, putting them right at the national average.

The girl in the box office seemed annoyed when I asked to see Mrs. Starks. She quickly looked me up and down and said I could wait "over there." I sat in the lobby, listening to my podcasts and watching people. The theater was busier than I thought it'd be—five to seven visitors every ten minutes for the hour I was there. Not too long after I'd sat down, I noticed a business-casually dressed pair request to see Donell, the other half of the ICE management team. After a few minutes of hemming and hawing, they were turned away. Donell wasn't in and neither was Alisa. I got the hint.

I returned a few days later for a proper interview. I'd seen her picture but still didn't recognize her when she dismounted from her SUV. "Are you Martine?" she called out to me from across the parking lot. I nodded and power walked towards her. We were both wearing magenta coats, hers was a fur, mine a parka. She opened up the theater, and we sat down in the lobby. A few employees were scattered around vacuuming the carpeted floors, stacking cups at the concession stand and organizing papers in the box office. Alisa is a petite woman on the cusp of fifty. She wears glasses and keeps her hair in a short Afro.

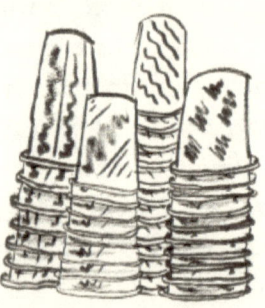

A stack of concession stand cups

She laughed a lot, with her head tilted back. She had told some of these stories many, many times. I could tell which parts she enjoyed sharing, like how they beat out Magic Johnson for the Chatham location. Other times she was matter-of-factly clearing up rumors. She was quick to point out that they were shut down for one day due to a technical default on a business loan.

Inner City Entertainment, Inc. was incorporated in 1994. Alisa was an advertising executive at Burrell Communications, and Donell worked as an investment banker. As 9-to-5-er's they had the entrepreneurial spirit, even if they didn't know what type of business they would open. "I thought it would be a restaurant because my grandmother, being from Louisiana, was an excellent cook," Alisa explained. While researching franchise opportunities they met the accountant for the Baldwin Theater, the first Black-owned, first-run movie theater in the country. He spoke disparagingly about franchises and encouraged them to start something on their own.

"We're still not thinking movie theaters," Alisa told me. One day they noticed a for-sale sign go up on the Hamilton Theater on 71st Street. "Because I'd been working for Burrell, a Black advertising agency, [I thought] what's the number one form of entertainment for Blacks outside of the home? It's going to the movies. There are no movie theaters in our communities. [We'd] just left Hollywood. I knew my husband would fall in love with the idea because it would tie him back to LA and Hollywood, even if it was vicariously," she said, connecting the dots.

Alisa saw that for-sale sign in 1991. After six years of hard work they opened three state-of-the-art multiplexes on the South and West sides of Chicago in November of 1997. Despite their desire to remain independent, the theaters were realized in collaboration with Cineplex Odeon. ICE wouldn't have received enough financing without the thirty-five year track record of their partner. Alisa confessed that the partnership was "challenging" over the years. "They didn't understand why they should do anything different. We've always perceived ourselves as a neighborhood theater, right or wrong, and we've got to better communicate that to the world... We're going to have the little jewelry lady [in the lobby] trying to make a dime because it's just who we are."

Shortly after ICE opened, Sony Loews—partners with their biggest competitor, Magic Johnson—aquired Cineplex. "Our dreams of expanding from market to market similar to the way he did kind of went away and our focus became on building Chicago," Alisa acknowledged solemnly. In 2000, Loews Cineplex went bankrupt and triggered a default on the Starks' multimillion-dollar loan. Their interest rates ballooned, and they decided to close everything but the Chatham location.

Their breadwinning site is in need of a few updates. While new theaters resemble nightclubs or high-end restaurants, ICE Chatham reminds me of the multiplexes that I frequented as a kid. It's painted with a palette of primary colors. Intimately sized movie posters are mounted on foamcore, with a corner modestly peeling off. "I told my husband the other day we were going to have to work on presentation so it feels a little different but that takes time, it takes capital to do all those things," she admitted. "We are hurting a bit by the fact that we didn't jump immediately on the 3D bandwagon." Nonetheless, they are prepared for the digital revolution. By 2012 all of their screens will be digital. At a $100,000 a pop, it's a big bet on their community.

When I asked how the movie theater was doing in a world of Netflix, On-Demand and torrents, Alisa sighed and began, "There are so few options in our community for entertainment and social events. We don't ski in great numbers. We don't raft in great numbers. We don't take major vacations to Europe, or Africa for that matter." Though my parents could have afforded it, I certainly never did any of those things until I was an adult. We had a thousand channels of cable programming, every video game system available and three new cars. We took a total of five family vacations during my youth. Twice to St. Louis, Missouri to visit my grandparents, twice to Las Vegas, Nevada to meet up with my aunts and uncles, and once to Berkeley, California for my oldest brother's college graduation. Our vacations were practical or functional, not social. We traveled when a child was born, a hip was replaced or the tickets were cheap. If my parents wanted to go on a family outing, we went to the movies.

I distinctly remember going to see *Forrest Gump* (1994)as a family. We saw it at a theater in a strip mall. I can imagine my mother doing a poor Bubba imitation both during and after the show. Talking during the film is characteristic of the Black movie going experience. According to Alisa, "We've got a greater social interaction in the movie theaters than others. It really becomes 'Oh girl, don't do that, don't do that.'" A few months ago on The Grio, an MSNBC news website for African-Americans, an article was titled "Why Some Blacks Prefer 'Whiter' Movie Theaters."[2] It was penned in response to an SNL skit in which actor Will Forte jokes about seeing *Precious* at the Magic Johnson Theater. The punch line: "The Black audience was talking to the screen a lot, so I couldn't understand ninety percent of it."

When I asked Alisa how she felt about ICE being labeled a Black movie theater, she expressed a pride that was tinged with frustration. "When you're grossing more than $5

2 Calypso, "Why Some Blacks Prefer 'Whiter' Movie Theaters."

million in total revenue for one facility, that's money – what we do primarily goes back to the black community." From their refreshments to their cleaning service to their insurance broker, ICE employs African-Americans. "I'm not saying I just do it because we're Black," she clarified, "But I make a conscious effort and a lot of people don't understand." Alisa is making a radical decision to invest in the inner city. Growing up in the sixties politicized her. "We have to see other people get engaged, start their own businesses, begin to figure out [that] we can all make a difference," she said optimistically.

Her irritation comes from the less altruistic patrons, bougie Blacks who would rather go downtown. "We're [thought of as] the 'theater in the hood,' the 'ghetto theater' ... that is the one disappointing thing. People get very different experiences when they come ... The experience a person has here is based on what movies they're coming to see." We discussed the different audiences that come to the theater and how they keep them apart. On the opening night of a popular movie the ICE lobby is filled with droves of teens. They have a senior special for Wednesday and Friday matinees. This keeps the elderly away from the youth. They try to schedule the dramas, the "For Colored Girls" crowd, in the early afternoon. On the first Thursday of every month they host Black World Cinema, a curated program of art house films that is organized by local filmmaker Floyd Webb. ICE also rents out their screens to independent filmmakers wanting a theatrical run.

When I tried to get Alisa to define what makes a movie Black, she wouldn't answer me. She thought the question was weird. She told me that if you're making a film with Black people in it you should target a Black audience. "That's where you ought to start because White people aren't coming to see your movie." She conceded that there might be a few White people interested in a Black-themed film ("There are some very liberal Whites—I like that. They're hipper than I am."). Even then she didn't think that Black people were a monolithic audience. We started talking about how to market a movie depending on which audience you were trying to reach. Are they your Blacks at the jazz festival or the art gallery? What channels do they watch and which radio stations do they listen to? I wanted to ask Alisa how she picked movies, but after our conversation I already knew. ICE screens movies that will sell tickets. I wanted there to be more to it than that. They pick up all of the blockbusters and round them out with Black themed flicks. There was no art to it. Alisa didn't even like the movies they played. She said she preferred independent film.

Still curious about how to define a Black movie theater I emailed National CineMedia, the in-theater advertising network for AMC Entertainment, Inc., Cinemark USA, Inc. and Regal Entertainment Group. Within minutes I was sent a list of all the African-American theaters in their range. I opened the spreadsheet hoping for answers. I was met with numbers. I ascertained that if more than eighteen percent of theatergoers were Black a site counted as an African-American theater. Eighteen percent seemed like an awfully low barrier to entry to me. It was like the one-drop rule for distribution.

According to marketing expert Seth Godin, demographics don't matter anymore. Psychographics rule the day. Demographics define race, gender, annual income, location and other quantifiable data. Psychographics corral motivations, interests, roles and the many intangibles that make us unique. Psychographics are more commonly referred to as taste. In his 1979 tome *Distinction*, pioneering sociologist Pierre Bourdieu revealed that taste has more to do with social structures than individual sagacity. He found that taste directly coincides with class. Last year Mark Grief, founder of the literary magazine N+1, wrote an essay analyzing the urban hipster through Bourdieu's lens. In it he maintains, "Bourdieu's innovation, applicable here, was to look beyond the traditional trappings of rich or poor to see battles of symbols ... traversing all society, reinforcing the class structure just as money did." [3]

N+1 published a book entitled *What Was The Hipster: A Sociological Investigation*, and blogger Patrice Evans contributed a piece about hip hop and "hipsterism." Although several authors acknowledged that the hipster was White, Evans was the only writer to consider what being a hipster (psychographics) meant for a Black person (demographics). "They say the issue of class is about the Haves and the Have-Nots, but that's only a small remove from the conversation of Us and Them," Evans writes. [4] He thinks "the term 'hipster' functions within a world of small distinctions where people don't want to name facts, and that it has some sort of repressed white-American sensibility in

3 Greif, "The Sociology of the Hipster."

4 *What Was The Hipster*, 104.

its essence."₅ In contemplating the Blipster, Evans decides that the Black hipster can still be attributed to Black popular culture. Demographics will always prevail, post-racial society or not. Bourdieu's research gives another dimension to my deliberation of race films. If social conditions like race undeniably inform taste, then there is an argument for a Black aesthetic.

5 Ibid., 105.

10. Black Movement

In my essays I've tried to describe how Blackness has been captured on film. I've meant to differentiate that process from any prescriptive agenda, but I am obsessed with finding the borders of both practices. I hesitated while writing this text several times, for many of the same reasons that make me pause whenever I'm asked about being a Black artist. I don't want to be representative of Black Artists. It's too much responsibility. I'm afraid that I'll fuck things up for everybody and that will be the end of Black Art.

On the plane back from our post-holiday vacation, my boyfriend read me a passage from *The Book of Tea* that declared, "Definition is always limitation—the "fixed" and "unchangeless" are but terms expressive of a stoppage of growth."[6] Being a "Black artist" comes with stipulations. The primary stipulation? That you be Black. Initially I resisted this perspective, but now I share Paul Gilroy's "anti-anti-essentialist" viewpoint. A "pro-essentialist" belief requires me to define Black, and gives me the authority to dismiss any signs of diversity as *not* Black. The anti-anti-essentialist asks what complex and contradictory forms Blackness might take. As a child nerd, a teenage punk, an art student and beyond, I've always had eclectic interests. Somehow my parents created the perfect

6 Okakura, *The Book of Tea*, 53.

symbiosis between forcing me to be a token—introducing me to disparate sounds, styles and conventions—and rooting me in Blackness. I learned who "we" are, what "we" eat, how "we" talk, but I was encouraged to renegotiate that construction to better fit me. The anti-anti-essentialist maintains an essentialist representation in relationship with others.

I've framed Blackness in relation to Whiteness because the film image situates them as negative and positive, respectively. This is tied to America's systematic neglect of slavery's legacy. Hollywood proposes an inverse relationship between the two races because there is too much at stake to compromise the audience. The industry drew a line in the sand many years ago and we haven't overcome it yet. In the 2008 documentary *The Black List*, Chris Rock recounts the advice his father used to give him, "[He] used to say 'You can't beat white people at anything, ever. But you can knock 'em out ... you can't let it go to the judge's decision, because you're gonna lose ... ' " The quote has stuck with me since I heard it. It demonstrates the inequality that permeates American society better than anything else I've been told. In Rock's comedy special *Kill The Messenger* (2008) he elaborates, "My house cost millions of dollars ... In my neighborhood there are four Black people. Hundreds of houses. Four Black people. Who are these Black people? There's me, Mary J. Blige, Jay-Z and Eddie Murphy. [We're] the only Black people in the whole neighborhood ... Do you know what the white man that lives next door to me does for a living? He's a fucking dentist." Black people are not a monolith, but the social condition of being

Black in America should be a unifying one. I don't really get to decide whether or not I'm a Black artist. Nor do I decide whether or not I'm a Black viewer. Why not subvert the charge of being Black into an identity that we own and explore the possibilities of such a platform?

For these possibilities to exist, the Black viewer/spectator must sit comfortably with the tension of "bad" portrayals, "unrealistic" experiences and/or a non-diasporic stylistic approach. Black audiences are also complicit in constructing race; perhaps even more so than the filmmaker, because the viewer/spectator is instructed to read the images and situate them in reality. We look to the movies like horoscopes confirming the best and worst things about us. My Aunt Linda, a long-time family friend, dismissed me and my brother's criticisms about Tyler Perry over dinner with a short wave of her hand. "Y'all don't like Madea because y'all didn't have that person on your block. You don't understand it," she said confidently, like a Taurus who'd just acknowledged her stubbornness. I'm not without blame. "Why are you watching this shit," I say arrogantly to my sister for watching *The Real Housewives of Atlanta* or reading Bossip, when I can easily get sucked into either media glut myself. I sometimes act like I only consume cinéaste fare.

Filmmakers have to understand that I'm looking for myself in their images. That is where my so-called taste comes from. Whatever delusions I have about myself, I want to see on-screen. I often joke that I'm not the target audience of any movie, so I console myself with a gritty drama that makes me sob uncontrollably. Or I go to the other extreme and watch a light-hearted comedy so hackneyed that I can

68

guess the plot. My favorite Black movies, *Killer of Sheep* (1977) and *A Good Day to be Black and Sexy* (2008), are neo-realist portraits of urban life.

Why argue about what's true and what's stereotype? Both representations are made within a context of subjection. After a presentation of an early draft of this text, a friend ventured that success for Black cinema will have arrived when a Black version of *Married with Children* hits and no one bats an eye. One day Blacks will be considered normal not because they are exceptional, but because they're mediocre. It will be the anti-*Cosby* moment. When that day comes, if it hasn't already, will I recognize it? As a conscious viewer it is my responsibility to allow Black filmmakers their freedom. It's my job to forgive them of the burden to uplift the race, so that they can do their work.

What work is that exactly? As a filmmaker, I'm still figuring that one out. Right now I document the moments in between bus rides and write down a lot of ideas. I read a few books each week and watch at least two movies. I don't make much, but that's okay. I'm still learning how to use my voice. Maybe that's why I can't speak when someone asks me what it means to be Black. I don't always know what it means. My protagonists are Black because that is the race that I imagine them to be. My works deals with race because I've never lived a day without running into it. My interest in Black culture is not political—it's fundamental. It's fantastic when those concerns intersect with the American subconscious, but it has nothing to do with my personal life. My life is one in which Black is a given. It doesn't need to be added, pre-fixed. In that place it's no longer important that I'm a Black artist and I can be a little more myself. I can be openly compromised. I can show what it's like to knock 'em out and what it's like to fail.

Selected Bibliography

Bogle, Donald. *Toms, Coons, Mulattoes, Mammies, and Bucks: An Interpretive History of Blacks in American Films*. Continuum International Publishing Group, 2001.

"Box Office Mojo." http://boxofficemojo.com/.

Calypso, Anthony. "Why Some Blacks Prefer 'Whiter' Movie Theaters." *The Grio*, May 28, 2010. http://www.thegrio.com/entertainment/why-some-blacks-prefer-whiter-movie-theaters.php.

CBS. "Tyler Perry's Amazing Journey to the Top." http://www.cbsnews.com/stories/2009/10/22/60minutes/main5410095_page4.shtml?tag=contentMain;contentBody.

CNN. "Mo'Nique On Award Nominations." http://majicatl.com/videos/carolblackmon/monique-on-award-nominations-im-appreciative-but-i-cant-let-it-drive-me-crazy/.

Cripps, Thomas. *Slow Fade to Black : The Negro in American Film, 1900-1942*. New York: Oxford University Press, 1993.

Dorsky, Nathaniel. *Devotional Cinema*. Tuumba Press, 2005.

Ebert, Roger. "B.A.P.S.." RogerEbert.com, March 28, 1997. http://rogerebert.suntimes.com/apps/pbcs.dll/article?AID=/19970328/REVIEWS/703280301/1023.

Greif, Mark. "The Sociology of the Hipster." *The New York Times*, November 12, 2010. http://www.nytimes.com/2010/11/14/books/review/Greif-t.html?_r=1.

———. *What was the hipster? : A Sociological Investigation*. New York: N+1 Foundation, 2010.

Grigely, Joseph. *Exhibition Prosthetics*. Sternberg Press and Bedford Press, 2009.

Guerrero, Ed. *Framing Blackness: The African American Image in Film*. Temple University Press, 1993.

Ice-T. "Ice-T's Rap on Blaxploitation - GetBack." *Get Back*. http://new.music.yahoo.com/blogs/getback/184/ice-ts-rap-on-blaxploitation.

Jafa, Arthur. "69." http://www.blackculturalstudies.org/a_jafa/69.html.

Jay, Timothy. "The Utility and Ubiquity of Taboo Words." Perspectives on Psychological Science 4, no. 2 (2009).

John, Derek. "Sounding Black." *Studio 360*, October 24, 2008.

Joshi, Amit. "Movie Advertising and the Stock Market Valuation of Studios: A Case of "Great Expectations"?." University of California Los Angeles, 2008.

Joyner, Will. "Staying Stubbornly True to a Writer's Vision." http://www.nytimes.com/1998/10/18/movies/film-staying-stubbornly-true-to-a-writer-s-vision.html?ref=oprahwinfrey&pagewanted=2.

Julius, Brittany. "In Which You're Listening To The Quiet Storm." *This Recording*, October 29, 2010. http://thisrecording.com/today/2010/10/29/in-which-youre-listening-to-the-quiet-storm.html.

Keyes, Allison. "Keep Your Hands Off The Hair." *Tell Me More*. National Public Radio, March 22, 2010.

Larry, George. "Black Preaching Myths – Is It Only For Black People?." http://www.soulpreaching.com/Black-preaching-myths-only-for-Black-people.

Massood, Paula J. "Which Way to the Promised Land?: Spike Lee's Clockers and the Legacy of the African American City." *African American Review* 35, no. 2 (July 1, 2001): 263-279.

McGinn, Dan. "Should Leaders Ever Swear?." *Harvard Business Review*, June 14, 2010. http://blogs.hbr.org/hbr/hbreditors/2010/06/do_good_leaders_swear.html.

Mercer, Kobena. "Black Hair/Style Politics." *New Formations*, no. Number 3 (Winter 1987).

Moon, Spencer. *Reel Black Talk: A Sourcebook of 50 American Filmmakers*. Greenwood Publishing Group, 1997.

Okakura, Kakuzō. *The Book of Tea*. Duffield, 1912.

Paperson, La. "The Postcolonial Ghetto: Seeing Her Shape and His Hand." *Berkeley Review of Education* 1, no. 1 (2010).

"Proenza Schouler." *Proenza Schouler / Special Projects / Act Da Fool.* http://www.proenzaschouler.com/shop/#/special-projects/act-da-fool/.

Smith, Cauleen. "Carousel Microcinema 4.2," Three Walls, Chicago, IL, August 26, 2010.

Smith, Valerie. *Representing Blackness: Issues in Film and Video.* Rutgers University Press, 1997.

Stewart, Jacqueline Najuma. *Migrating to the Movies: Cinema and Black Urban Modernity.* University of California Press, 2005.

Sutton, Bob. "Strategic Use of Swearing in the Workplace." *Bob Sutton*, June 18, 2010. http://bobsutton.typepad.com/my_weblog/2010/06/strategic-use-of-swearing-in-the-workplace.html.

The Making of Jive Talk from Airplane!, 2009. http://www.youtube.com/watch?v=7fkZdz4Vz10&feature=youtube_gdata_player.

Weinraub, Bernard. "'Beloved' Tests Racial Themes At Box Office; Will This Winfrey Film Appeal to White Audiences? - New York Times." http://www.nytimes.com/1998/10/13/movies/beloved-tests-racial-themes-box-office-will-this-winfrey-film-appeal-white.html?ref=oprahwinfrey&pagewanted=1.

White, Armond. "Pride & Precious." http://www.nypress.com/article-20554-pride-precious.html.

Williams, Patricia J. "Racial Ventriloquism." *The Nation*, June 17, 1999. http://web.archive.org/web/20060920011550/http://www.thenation.com/doc/19990705/williams.

Willis, Holly. "Art Sims." *AIGA | the professional association for design.* http://www.aiga.org/content.cfm/design-journeys-art-sims.

Film & Television References

A Good Day to be Black and Sexy. Dir. Dennis Dortch. 1976 Experience, 2008.

Act Da Fool. Dir. Harmony Korine. Proenza Schouler, 2010.

Airplane!. Dir. Jim Abrahams, David Zucker and Jerry Zucker. Paramount Pictures, 1980.

B*A*P*S. Dir. Robert Townsend. New Line Cinema, 1997.

Barbershop 2: Back in Business. Dir. Kevin Roney Sullivan. Metro-Goldwyn-Mayer and Cubevision, 2004.

Barbershop. Dir. Tim Story. Metro-Goldwyn-Mayer and Cubevision, 2002.

Beauty Shop. Dir. Billie Woodruff. Metro-Goldwyn-Mayer and State Street Pictures, 2005.

Belly. Dir. Hype Williams. Big Dog Films, 1998.

Beloved. Dir. Jonathan Demme. Touchstone Pictures, 1998.

Boyz n the Hood. Dir. John Singleton. Columbia Pictures, 1991.

Burlesque. Dir. Steve Antin. De Line Pictures, 2010.

Chris Rock: Kill the Messenger – London, New York, Johannesburg. CR Enterprises and Funny Business Productions, 2008.

Cotton Comes to Harlem. Dir. Ossie Davis. Formosa Productions, 1970.

Do The Right Thing. Dir. Spike Lee. 40 Acres & A Mule Filmworks, 1989.

Doug. Jumbo Pictures and Nickelodeon Network,1991-1994.

Faster. Dir. George Tillman Jr.. TriStar Pictures, 2010.

For Colored Girls. Dir. Tyler Perry. Lionsgate and 34th Street Films, 2010.

Forrest Gump. Dir. Robert Zemeckis. Paramount Pictures, 1994.

Friday. Dir. F. Gary Gray. New Line Cinema, 1995.

Good Hair. Dir. Jeff Stilson. Chris Rock Entertainment and HBO Films, 2009.

Guess Who. Dir. Kevin Rodney Sullivan. Columbia Pictures, 2005.

Guess Who's Coming to Dinner. Dir. Stanley Kramer. Columbia Pictures, 1967.

Harry Potter and the Deathly Hallows – Part 1. Dir. David Yates. Warner Bros. Pictures, 2010.

Killer of Sheep. Dir. Charles Burnett. 1981.

Lean on Me. Dir. John G. Avildsen. Warner Bros. Pictures, 1989.

Mackin' Ain't Easy. Dir. Laura Nix. Automat Pictures, 2002.

Malcolm X. Dir. Spike Lee. 40 Acres & A Mule Filmworks, Largo International and JVC Entertainment Networks, 1992.

Married with Children. Sony Pictures Entertainment, 1987-1997.

Megamind. Dir. Tom McGrath. Dreamworks Animation, 2010.

Menace II Society. Dir. Albert Hughes and Allen Hughes. New Line Cinema, 1993.

New Jack City. Dir. Mario Van Peebles. Warner Bros. Pictures, 1991.

Next Friday. Dir. Steve Carr. New Line Cinema and Cubevision, 2000.

Poetic Justice. Dir. John Singleton. Columbia Pictures, 1993.

Precious. Dir. Lee Daniels. Lee Daniels Entertainment, 2009.

Richard Pryor Live on the Sunset Strip. Dir. Joe Layton. Columbia Pictures, 1982.

Scarface. Dir. Brian De Palma. Universal Pictures 1983.

Schindler's List. Dir. Steven Spielberg. Universal Pictures, 1993.

School Daze. Dir. Spike Lee. 40 Acres & A Mule Filmworks and Columbia Pictures, 1988.

Sister Act 2. Dir. Bill Duke. Touchstone Pictures, 1993.

Sister Act. Dir. Bill Duke. Touchstone Pictures, 1992.

Skyline. Dir. Colin Strause and Greg Strause. Black Monday Film Services, 2010.

Something New. Dir. Sanaa Hamri. Gramercy Pictures, 2006.

Space is the Place. Dir. John Coney. North American Star System, 1974.

Star Wars: Episode 1 - The Phantom Menace. Dir. George Lucas. Lucasfilm, 1999.

Sweet Sweetback's Badasssss Song. Dir. Melvin Van Peebles. Yeah, 1971.

Tangled. Dir. Nathan Greno and Byron Howard. Walt Disney Pictures, 2010.

The Best Man. Dir. Malcolm D. Lee. 40 Acres & A Mule Filmworks, 1999.

The Black List: Volume One. Dir. Timothy Greenfield-Sanders. Perfect Day Films, 2008.

The Bodyguard. Dir. Mick Jackson. Warner Bros. Pictures, 1992.

The Brothers. Dir. Gary Hardwick. Screen Gems, 2001.

The Color Purple. Dir. Steven Spielberg. Warner Bros. Pictures, 1985.

The Cosby Show. National Broadcasting Company and Bill Cosby, 1984-1992.

The Fresh Prince of Bel-Air. NBC Productions and Quincy Jones Entertainment, 1990-1996.

The Fullness of Time. Dir. Cauleen Smith. Paul Chan and Creative Time, 2008.

The Homesteader. Dir. Oscar Micheaux. The Micheaux Book and Film Company, 1919.

The Jacksons: An American Dream. Dir. Karen Arthur. Motown Productions, 1992.

The Mack. Dir. Michael Campus. Harbor Productions, 1973.

The Men Who Stare at Goats. Dir. Grant Heslov. BBC Films, 2009.

The Next Three Days. Dir. Paul Haggis. Lionsgate, 2010.

The Sandlot. Dir. David M. Evans. Twentieth Century Fox Film Corporation, 1993.

The Warrior's Way. Dir. Sngmoo Lee. Culture Unplugged Studios, 2010.

Unstoppable. Dir. Tony Scott. Twentieth Century Fox Film Corporation, 2010.

Waiting to Exhale. Dir. Forest Whitaker. Twentieth Century Fox Film Corporation, 1995.

Why Did I Get Married. Dir. Tyler Perry. Lions Gate Films and The Tyler Perry Company, 2007.

Within Our Gates. Dir. Oscar Micheaux. The Micheaux Book and Film Company, 1920.

Thanks to Lauren Anderson, Marco Kane Braunschweiler, Steffani Jemison, Katie Lennard, Lee Lynch, Alisa Starks and The Syms Family.

ISBN: 978-0-9833815-1-8

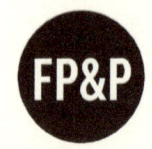

future plan and program

Future Plan and Program
http://futureplanandprogram.com

Please direct inquiries to:
thefuture@futureplanandprogram.com

Series editor: Steffani Jemison
Series designer: Sebastian Civarolo
Design: Purpure Co. with Sebastian Civarolo
Illustrations: Lauren Anderson

Future Plan and Program was incubated in 2010-2011 by Project Row Houses.

Acknowledgements: Danielle Burns, Justin Cavin, Aisen Chacin, Ashley Clemmer-Hoffman, Cheryl Flores, Quincy Flowers, Hannah Ireland, Philip Jemison, Steven Jemison, Rick Lowe, Jasmine Jamillah Mahmoud, Phyllis McCallum, Solkem N'Gangbet, Michael Peranteau, Nikki Pressley, Linda Shearer, Martine Syms, Michael Kahlil Taylor, and Julie Thomson.

Future Plan and Program was generously funded in part by the following individuals: Kerry Inman & Denby Auble, John Roberson & John Blackmon, Danielle Antoinette Burns, Justin Cavin, Jereann Chaney, Melody Clark, Ashley Clemmer Hoffman & Brendan Hoffman, Phyllis L. McCallum and Steven Jemison, Joey Romano & Nicole Laurent, Victoria Thomas McGhee, Scott Sawyer & Michael Peranteau, Gregory & Diane Schultz, Leigh & Reggie Smith, and Rebecca Trahan. Special thanks to Jill Whitten & Robert Proctor.

Funding for Steffani Jemison's residency at Project Row Houses was provided by: The National Endowment for the Arts, the City of Houston through the Houston Arts Alliance, Houston Endowment Inc., The Brown Foundation, The Kresge Foundation, The Andy Warhol Foundation for the Visual Arts, and the Texas Commission on the Arts. Steffani Jemison's residency was part of a collaboration with the Core Program at the Glassell School of Art of the Museum of Fine Arts Houston.